Conflicted Generations

A Study of Conflict in the lives of Abraham, Isaac and Jacob

Conflicted Generations

A Study of Conflict in the lives of Abraham, Isaac and Jacob

Tom Wilson

Contents

Preface

The Bible is filled with stories of conflict, which is hardly surprising as it is filled with human stories, and wherever there are people, you will always find disputes, arguments and disagreements. Think for a moment about the very first human beings. Adam and Eve quickly got into an argument, as soon as they had eaten from the tree which God had told them to stay away from. After they had eaten, they realised they were naked, and hid themselves, out of fear and shame. The Lord God walks in the garden, and calls out to them, wanting to speak with them. They explain why they are hiding, and the Lord asks them the source of their recently acquired knowledge. When they admit they have disobeyed God's command, the recriminations start. Adam blames both God and Eve—'The *woman you gave me* led me to this,' and Eve blames the serpent. Neither is prepared to take responsibility, both blame others, and the seeds of conflict are sown.

Their sons fare no better. Abel keeps flocks, Cain farms the land. We have no reason to suppose either is bad at his job. All we know is that when both brought an offering of the best of what they had produced, Abel's was acceptable to the Lord, but Cain's was rejected. The Bible does not give us God's reasoning, and it would be foolish for us to speculate. I assume that it was simply for Cain and Abel to learn to trust Yahweh's revelation of himself. They had to learn that God's ways are not our ways, that he is bigger than us and decides what is acceptable and what is not.

This idea, that Cain especially had to learn to trust the Lord and not rely on his own strength, is seen in the discussion that takes place between the Lord and Cain after Cain's sacrifice has been rejected. The Lord questions Cain, asking him why he is so upset, and warns him that sin is crouching at the door of his heart, like a tiger poised to leap and kill. Cain must drive away the temptation before it gets too close and devours him. Sadly Cain is unable to resist, and the result is violent conflict. Presumably his jealousy of his brother got the better of him. Cain persuades his brother to go with him into the field, onto Cain's territory, as it were, and there he kills Abel. Swift and bloody jealousy, conflict brought about by a desire to better one's brother.

These stories could continue, but the point is clear. Conflict is inevitable. Human beings always have and always will engage in some form of conflict. Rather than pretend we can avoid all conflict, we should accept this fact. If we do not, all that happens is unhealthy conflict: big arguments over tiny differences, huge upsets for small problems. Conflict is inevitable.

While it may be true that there will always be disagreements amongst us, that does not mean destructive disagreement is definitive. There is potential for good that can come out of conflict, if it is handled in appropriate ways. We may have arguments, but they are not always unhealthy or destructive. To give an everyday example, a decision about where to go and what to do on a family holiday can be a real opportunity for children to grow in taking responsibility and leadership, or it can be a source of real upset and strife. We will always disagree about all kinds of things, and rather than pretending we do not, it is much healthier to work out how to put all that energy and creativity into good use.

The aim of the five chapters that follow is to offer some suggestions for how to transform conflict from something that is destructive and draining into something positive and life-giving. Each section has three elements: a reflection on a Bible story which includes some conflict; a story that picks up on the Bible reflection; and questions for discussion or personal reflection. All the Biblical reflections are drawn from a particular section of the Bible, the stories of Abraham, Isaac and Jacob. Each experienced a lot of conflict, and I have drawn five lessons from their lives. There is plenty more that could have been said, but hopefully these will be enough to begun to help us see conflict differently, not as something to avoid but as a positive opportunity for change and growth.

Abraham

When he made the black and white film *The Gospel according to St Matthew*, Italian director Pier Paolo Pasolini decided to only use the text of the gospel itself, since he felt that 'images could never reach the poetic heights of the text.' The result is an eerie and challenging film. In one early scene, two men are silently cleaning nets by the shore of a lake. A solitary figure walks up to them and simply says, 'Come, follow me, and I will send you out to fish for people.' Silently they follow. The three walk to two others, who join them. A single sentence, no argument, no discussion, just obedience; four people follow Jesus. Is that exactly how Jesus called them and calls us? Is it always that simple?

The decision to follow the Lord's call is a decision that both resolves and leads to conflict. It resolves it in the sense that the conflict between your will for your life and God's will for your life is over, at least temporarily. It leads to conflict in the sense that God's plan can put you in opposition to human plans, to other people's agendas or even to your own personal plan for your life. Abraham was someone who made that choice, and my discussion of conflict and the life of faith will begin with the way in which he made that choice and the impact the choice had on his whole family. I will examine four critical incidents in Abraham's life to illustrate the process of making that choice. They are: his decision to leave Ur; his dilemma over how to describe Sarah; his covenant with Yahweh; and his almost sacrifice of his son, Isaac. Each are steps on the journey of deciding to walk by faith, not sight, and all can be seen as part of the struggle for Abraham to follow the Lord's will, not his own.

Leaving the familiarity of home was a vital first step. Quite whether as loaded a word as 'conflict' is relevant to that decision is a moot point, but it cannot have been an easy choice to make. Abram, as he was known at the time, was aware he was no longer living where he was supposed to be. How he knew that I cannot say, but the Bible is clear that the Lord called him, and told him to leave Ur and head for Canaan, taking his family and all his livestock with him (Genesis 12:1-9). The journey would be filled with danger. A pastoral nomad like Abram stood to loose his wealth, as his animals might have died or been stolen on the journey. But more than that, he stood to loose all contact with his extended family. There was no easy means of communication and travel was dangerous. He or his wife might have died on the journey or even in Canaan itself. Where was the sense in leaving home and going to an unknown land, just because an unknown God told him to? This is the choice that we all face: to remain in the security and familiarity of running our own lives, or to step out in faith. The conflict is the conflict of faith: my way, or God's? We all face the choice, and the question is whether it will be said of us as of him; 'Abram believed God and it was credited to him as righteousness' (Genesis 15:6).

The fact that this was not an easy decision is borne out in the events which follow that first decision to leave Ur and head towards Canaan. Famine forces Abram and Sarai to take refuge in Egypt, but when they do, fear beats faith in the conflict for peace of mind. Abram introduces Sarai as his sister, nothing more, neglecting to mention they are married. He is worried that because Sarai is so beautiful, if he is known as her husband, Pharaoh will have him killed in order to take her for himself. If he simply says he is her brother, then perhaps Pharaoh will at least spaeak with Abram before making a move on Sarai. But even though he does not trust in Yahweh's protection, that is still present, as Pharaoh's attraction for Sarai is halted by a

2

dream, warning him off (Genesis 12:10-20). Abram struggles to trust in Yahweh's care, which is why I have described his journey of faith as one filled with conflict. There is a battle raging for Abram's loyalty, a battle between Yahweh and self-control. Yahweh does triumph, but it is not a straightforward process. The nature of the struggle is clear from the fact that Abram does not learn the lesson of his first failure of faith. He repeats the same ruse years later, suggesting to Abimelech, as to Pharaoh, that Sarah is just his sister, not his wife as well (Genesis 20). There was some truth in Abraham's statement, as Genesis 20:12 points out that Abraham and Sarah had the same father, but different mothers. But being sparing with the truth is still a sign of lack of trust. In the conflict between fear and faith, fear is gnawing away at the certainty of faith. Pressure pushes Abraham into foolish decisions, ones he later regrets.

I am not using this example to attack Abraham but rather to give us a realistic picture of the conflict of faith. Each day we try to live loyal to Jesus is a day in which we ourselves face that same conflict. The danger may not be as acute or as immediate, but it is just as real. The Christian life is a challenge, not because God is not worthy of our faith, nor because there is insufficient evidence for trusting his promises, but rather because human beings are so curved in on themselves, so bent over in self-absorbed delusion, that the process of straightening out is a long and difficult one. The Lord asks us to trust him with both the big and the small things in life, and this is a difficult habit to get into. It is the one we were originally made for, but need to get back into the groove of.

Abram received a covenant to help him stand tall and fix his eyes on Yahweh, and anyone who chooses to walk the same path becomes part of the fulfillment of that promise (Genesis 15; 17). The promise was that he would be father to a great nation, although not a nation in the sense of an ethnicity so much as a people of faith, distinguished by their total reliance on God, rather than by geographical or political boundaries. That covenant came in two parts. In Genesis 15, the issue at hand is the continuity of the promise. The Lord has promised Abraham and his descendants will be a blessing to the world, but he has no children. The Lord promises a son, and seals the promise with sacrifices, with darkness and with fire. The promise is confirmed in Genesis 17. The sign of circumcision is given to Abraham and his sons as a sacrament, an outward and visible sign of the inward, invisible reality of being one of God's chosen ones. We no longer have that same sacrament, but we who are heirs of Abraham through faithful obedience remain God's children. This covenant, affirmed initially to Abraham, and re-affirmed down the generations, is the solution to the conflict of faith, calling us to lives of obedience and trust, not unquestioning or blind faith, but resolved on the basis of a knowledge of history, of compelling evidence of how God has worked in the past, as well as our own and other people's personal experience to rely upon the Lord.

The name changes of Genesis 17 exemplify this. Abram, 'exalted father,' becomes Abraham, 'father of many,' and Sarai becomes Sarah, simply a change in pronunciation, but retaining the meaning 'princess.' The significance of the change in name lies in the fact that names were believed to indicate a person's character and destiny; thus with God's promise comes the reminder of God's action. Abraham will be reminded of his faithful God every time someone addresses him.

For Abraham, the decision to walk by faith is reinforced by the covenant that Yahweh makes with him. A covenant is a solemn promise, a certain guarantee of continued relationship and in this case of land and descendants. The covenant is sealed by the blood of animal sacrifices, and the presence of God symbolised by fire. I think for Abraham this must have been one of the moments which confirmed his decision to trust everything to the Lord. He had risked much, and here was a firm foundation upon which he could establish and build his house of faith. Having built on solid foundations, Abraham was prepared to trust everything to the Lord.

We see this in Abraham's discussion with the Lord over the fate of Sodom and Gomorrah (Genesis 18:16-33). The Lord has appeared to Abraham and Sarah, and reminded them again of the promised birth of a son (Genesis 18:1-15). Once they have eaten, Abraham and the Lord walk towards Sodom. The Lord makes clear his decision to judge both Sodom and Gomorrah, and Abraham pleads with him, arguing that any righteous people in the city should be given the chance to escape. The text does not give any indication of tone of voice, but I imagine Abraham pleading and bantering with God, confident, but not cocky; certain, but not presumptuous; slightly cheeky, but not overstepping the mark. There is horse trading in the numbers of righteous people needed to save the city. Fifty? Forty-five? Forty? Thirty? Twenty? Ten? At this point, the conversation stops. Abraham knows when he has gone far enough. He has fought, but now is at peace. He trusts divine justice, even if he does not know the outcome. In the end, only Lot and his two daughters are saved.

The quality of Abraham's faith is most clearly expressed in his choice to offer Isaac. Isaac was a son born to Abraham in his old age, and the circumstances of his birth will be the subject of the next chapter. The crucial point for this discussion is that Isaac was the son of the promise, the one through whom the promised generations of the faithful would come. And so when Yahweh called Abraham to offer Isaac as a sacrifice, it was a test of Abraham's faith in Yahweh's word. A test which Abraham passed because he believed Yahweh would keep his word.

God calls to Abraham, and tells him to take his son to the region of Moriah, and sacrifice him there as a burnt offering to God (Genesis 22:2). Abraham complies; setting out with Isaac and two servants. When they get to the base of the chosen mountain, he orders the servants to wait, while he and Isaac go on. The conversation shows the depth of Abraham's faith.

5

He instructs his servants: 'Stay here with the donkey, while I and the boy go over there. We will worship and then we will come back to you.'

As they climb, Isaac notes the lack of an animal to sacrifice, and when he raises this issue, his father replies, 'God himself will provide the lamb for the burnt offering, my son.'

Both times Abraham remains confident. He expects to come back with Isaac to his servants, and he expects the Lord to provide a sacrifice, which is exactly what he does.

Isaac is bound and placed on the wood, Abraham's knife is raised to sacrifice his son, and then the voice speaks from heaven: 'Abraham! Abraham! ...Do not lay a hand on the boy. Do not do anything to him. Now that I know that you fear God, because you have not withheld from me your son, your only son' (Genesis 22:11-12).

Abraham looks up, and there in the thicket is a ram, caught by his horns, which Abraham catches and offers as a sacrifice to the Lord. Faith has triumphed, fear is defeated, and the conflict is over.

Some might object that the idea of child sacrifice is barbaric and cannot be associated with the loving God revealed to us supremely in Jesus Christ. It is certainly true that the Lord repeatedly condemns child sacrifice through the prophets, but it is also true that since he is the author of life, then we cannot fully comprehend his ways. For me, the test Abraham faced was over belief in the Lord's power over death. If Isaac was the son through whom the covenant of blessing would be fulfilled, and the Lord called for Isaac to be sacrificed, then the Lord must be the one to raise him to life. As I noted above, Abraham believed God, and it was credited to him as righteousness. The earlier struggles had given way to firm faith. The conflict was over, peace reigned. The peace that only the Lord brings, not simply the absence of conflict, but the presence of God, complete trust in his plan. The lesson Abraham teaches us of a growth in reliance on God, of conflict giving way to certainty.

The challenge to us is over the conflict of faith. How far have you walked down this road? How complete is your surrender to God? This is not really a question of whether you have decided to become a missionary or church worker, but whether you have decided that your agenda for your life should be surrendered to God's. An entirely fictional example may help explain.

Helen is in her early forties, married with two children, both in primary school. She works in administration, nothing glamorous, just a job to pay the bills. Her husband is also an office worker. They met at university, in the Christian union. They've talked occasionally about 'going overseas for mission work,' but normally only when life was either unbelievably dull or unbelievably stressful. It has always been an exercise in spotting greener grass somewhere the other side of an imaginary fence, rather than any sort of a response to a call from God. For Helen, there are so many conflicts of faith: trusting for her children's future faith and life prospects, worrying about the cost of living, stress at work, the realisation that not all her childhood dreams are likely to ever become reality. Her husband is equally conflicted. He has so far failed to realise his dream of becoming a great musician. He is competent, but not sparkling, and will never get the major record deal he used to dream of. Work is fine, but there is no likelihood of making the serious money he secretly wishes for. The family are comfortable, provided they are careful, but there are always worries about money. Sometimes he feels a failure as a husband, doubting he lives up to the idea of the Christian man he wants to be. There are so many uncertainties, so many concerns. Walking by faith does not mean leaving for Peru, but recognising that while the way ahead may not be clearly sign posted, the Lord does have it under control.

The question this leaves for each of us is, are we walking by faith or by sight? That is to say, do we trust the Lord's plans and purposes for our lives, or are we determined to remain in control ourselves, to try and manage things our own way? I have tried to show how Abraham began to trust the Lord, and followed his call to leave Ur and go to Canaan. There was a process of growing in faith, a need to overcome the conflict between faith in God and self-determination. We all face that conflict each and every day, and should learn from Abraham's example of faithful trust and wholehearted obedience. In a sense, faith is a bit like abseiling. If you trust the rope and step out boldly, it is easy. If you fear the rope, crouch and slip, then it is terrifying. We all need to learn to step out confidently, to walk tall and live out our faith.

Story

'I don't know, I just don't know what to think about it all,' Chris sighed, scratching his head with his left hand. 'I mean, I guess I believe that there is a God, but this whole dying for your sins thing. Doesn't make any sense to me.'

This was by no means a new discussion. Chris and Harry had been friends for a number of years, and Chris had always been fascinated by Harry's Christian faith. The thing that had struck him most forcibly was the fact that Harry so rarely swore. There was that one memorable time when the office photocopier had broken. Harry had spent a frustrating fifteen minutes trying to make it work, and when it had chewed up the umpteenth copy of the minutes he needed for a meeting that was due to start in about two minutes, Harry had been reduced to cursing the machine in the choicest of language as he kicked it in frustration.

But 'photocopiergate,' as Chris liked to call it, had been the exception which had proved the rule of Harry's clean mouth. He was a regular guy in the office, worked hard, looked out for his colleagues, but did not suck up to the boss unnecessarily.

Harry was a fan of real ale, and was happy to enjoy one after—never during—work. An all round decent chap.

One Thursday evening in the Golden Hart, the pub next door to work, as they savoured a local golden special brew, Chris had asked Harry whether he believed in God. Chris' niece had been christened the week before, and he had endured (definitely not enjoyed) a slightly dreary service in which the vicar who had poured the water barely smiled, never mind looked happy to be a follower of Jesus. Chris was trying to work out why someone would do a job they did not seem to enjoy in the least.

'I mean, it makes no sense to me,' he explained, 'If the guy believed in God, then surely christening a baby is a great thing to do? It means more people in the church, more support and all that.'

'Well I guess so,' replied Harry. 'Yeah, I do believe in God. But I have to admit that sometimes when I go to church, and we see a family come for a christening, a family who we've never seen before, and never do again after the service, then it does make you wonder. Maybe this vicar was just a bit fed up of people coming, taking up his time, and then going away, never to be seen again. But even so, I think you're right. The guy could at least have smiled.'

'Yeah, completely. I mean I do believe in God. Its just this whole dying for your sins thing that I am not so sure about. I mean, am I even that bad a person?'

And so the first of many conversations on the theme of sin and forgiveness began. Chris and Harry soon discovered that they had two, slightly different, views about the mean of 'sin' and 'forgiveness.' For Chris, sin meant really bad stuff, like murder and rape. Since he had never done either, that meant he was not really sinful, and so did not need forgiving. For Harry, sin meant ignoring God, trying to run your own life. Since he freely admitted he did that, he did think he was sinful, and did think that he needed to be forgiven. It took them several months to agree on these two definitions, and even longer for Chris to start to understand Harry's point of view.

They were back in the Golden Hart, relaxing near a log fire one chilly February Wednesday evening. 5:30pm, work just finished, a swift drink before catching the train home.

'Like I said Harry, I think I get what you mean that sin is not just hugely bad stuff. That fancying Tracy could be sinful.'

Harry smiled. Tracy, their receptionist, a leggy blond twenty-something, was the subject of the fantasies of several of the office staff. She was also happily married, with a one-year old, just back from maternity leave.

'Yeah, I think having an affair with a new mum is probably a bad idea. And even thinking about it is not especially helpful.'

'True, true,' Chris conceded. 'So what you're saying is, anything I think that's wrong is as bad as if I actually did it?'

'Pretty much,' confirmed Harry. 'The whole point is, the Christian understanding of sin is less to do with behaviour, and more to do with attitude. Am I living for myself, or am I living for God. That's what makes it so hard, and that's why I have to admit that I've failed.'

'I don't think you fail. You're a decent bloke,' countered Chris.

'Possibly, possibly. But I know what I sometimes think. I may not say it, but photocopiergate has happened in my head on more than one occasion. And there are times when I get really grumpy with the kids for no reason other than they're having fun, and I want peace and quiet.'

'Don't we all?'

'That's exactly my point,' said Harry, taking another sip of his pint. 'We all mess up. We all keep choosing to do our own thing rather than God's thing. That's the struggle.'

The debate went on. Chris was still not sure he was ready to call himself a sinner, and fifteen minutes later, having both finished their drinks, they headed out towards the station together.

'Think of it like this,' said Harry, making one final attempt to get his point across, 'You're about to go and get on a train, right?'

'You bet. Its definitely time for home.'

'Yeah it is. Well, the train only ever goes on its tracks, right?'

'I hope so!'

Harry smiled. 'And we're not like that. We don't go where we are supposed to. We're like a train that's jumped its tracks and is running free on the road. Chaos. Destruction. Disaster. What choosing to follow God is basically about is getting back on the tracks, and running as you were supposed to.'

'I see what you mean. I'll think about it,' said Chris. 'But the thing I really want to know is, who do you think will win tonight in the Champion's League?'

Their conversation drifted to football as their train took them to their respective stations. Once home, Harry, having greeted his wife, and helped finish making dinner, sat down with her to eat. They were only recently married, and were still enjoying the life of a childless couple, although plans for a family were in formation.

The conversation drifted around what they had both been doing that day, landing finally on Harry's after work trip to the Golden Hart. 'The thing with Chris is,' said Harry, as he twirled spaghetti onto his fork, 'is that he just isn't ready to give up the fight to run his own life.'

'Well, we know what that's like,' smiled Sue. 'I mean, we kept stressing at uni, didn't we, about whether we were doing exactly the right thing. Were we taking the courses the Lord wanted us to? Were we looking at the right job?'

'Yeah,' smiled Harry. 'Do you remember how long I spent agonising about which of the two accountancy jobs to apply for, and then I didn't even get through the first round of either application. Two days of prayer and angst, and the answer was simple. Neither.'

'Well that's the thing about following God's call, isn't it?' said Sue, balancing sauce onto her fork, 'often times you don't know if you've got it right, but you just try to follow as best you can.'

'You're right. I think the hardest part for me was admitting I had screwed up my life and needed Jesus to sort it out. Now I know I'm a screw-up, the rest is easy.'

Sue smiled, 'You're a lovely screw-up, though. Chris'll get there in the end. It sounds like he's on his way in the right direction. Its not an easy battle, and we all want to pretend we're in charge of our own lives for as long as possible.'

'I guess.' Harry said, loading a final forkful. 'Learning to trust the Lord in everything isn't easy. I know I'm not all that good at it, and have loads still to learn.'

'We all do. What do you reckon the Lord wants us to do this evening?'

Harry closed his eyes, then opened them and grinned, 'I think he is leading you to do the washing up, and me to lie on the sofa watching the footie?'

'Really?' pouted Sue in mock indignation. 'I had a vision of you washing up and me having a long relaxing hot bath.'

'Well in that case, we're both washing up I guess. Trust and obey, for there's no other way.' Harry began humming as he gathered plates and headed into the kitchen.

Questions for discussion

Sometimes you just have to keep listening. Often, this most simple and basic step is all that is needed to help people come to a resolution of the conflict they are facing. In the story above, Harry spends a lot of time listening to Chris. He does, of course, also talk. He explains his faith, but only when Chris is ready to listen. My aim in telling this short story about Chris was to emphasise the point that the decision to follow Christ is, in fact, a daily conflict, a continual struggle in which we choose to ignore our own agenda and submit to Christ's instead. Abraham is our father in faith because he continually chose to surrender his agenda and submit to Yahweh's. He sets us the example we are called to follow.

1. How important is it for you to be listened to? How do you feel when you suspect someone is not actually listening to you?

2. How easy do you find it to listen to others?

3. How easy do you find it to listen to God's call on your life, and surrender your own plans to that call?

   Read Genesis 22

1. How did God's command in verse two challenge Abraham?

2. How does Abraham show his faith? (Note also Hebrews 11:17-18).

3. What situations do you face that challenge your faith in God? How do you face up to those challenges?

Hagar and Sarah

Returning to Hagar and Sarah may seem like a step backwards after discussing Abraham's entire life in the previous chapter, but it is such a pivotal story that I want to examine it separately. The conflict that has resulted from Hagar's and Sarah's children still plays out today, and so it is important to give it adequate space in a study on conflict in the lives of the Patriarchs and today.

There are many sides to any story, and what I would like to illustrate here is how different, conflicting accounts of the same event grow up and take root. The differences here are between the Judaeo-Christian account and the Islamic account of Abraham's children. My concern is not so much with truth (in the sense of arguing for my perspective that the Judaeo-Christian account is right and the Islamic one wrong), as with letting the competing stories jostle for space to illustrate the conflict over origins that still dominates our world today.

The account in Genesis 16 is like this. Sarai knows that Abram has been promised offspring, but she also knows that she has been unable to have any children, and it is now a number of years since the promise was made. So she suggests a solution, which is in fact more of a problem in the long term. Sarai thinks it would be sensible for Abram to sleep with her servant girl, Hagar, and have a child that way. It is essentially a crude experiment. The infertility that lies at the root of their failure to conceive lies either with Abram or Sarai. If Abram can impregnate another woman, then clearly his fertility is not the issue. Abram, happy to do what his wife suggests, duly has sex with Hagar, and she becomes pregnant.

The reason I think this idea was less of a solution and more of a problem is because of what happens next. Hagar was able to have a baby after having intercourse with Abram, making it clear that the issue of fertility was Sarai's, not Abram's. In a culture where having an heir was vital for social standing, being able to conceive when your mistress could not placed the balance of power more in Hagar's hands than Sarai's. So, entirely predictably, Hagar becomes proud, Sarai jealous, and she complains to Abram.

Abram, sensibly or foolishly, absolves himself of all responsibility, reasoning that it was Sarai's idea in the first place, so what happens to Hagar is also up to her. Sarai treats Hagar harshly, and Hagar flees for her life, preferring the uncertain danger of the desert to the sure pain of servitude. Remember she is pregnant, alone, vulnerable. Running away can often seem attractive, but can also lead to pain, as it does in this case. Hagar is in danger in the desert; at risk of starvation, dehydration, and maybe of attack. But the Lord sees her distress and sends an angel to care for her. Her main need is for water, and that is provided for her. The angel then explains what her future holds; that Abram will care her, the boy will be called *Ishmael* (God hears), and that he will grow up to be the father of a strong nation. Then comes the key point: 'He will be a wild donkey of a man; his hand will be against everyone and everyone's hand against him, and he will live in hostility towards all his brothers' (Genesis 16:12). Ishmael, born out of conflict, will live in conflict all of his life. Hagar remembers the Lord's provision by naming the well *Beer-lahai-roi*, which means 'the well of the Living One who sees me.'

The story does not end there, and just as the angel foretold, there is conflict between Ishmael and Isaac (Genesis 21:1-21). Once Isaac has been born to Sarah, she is again dissatisfied with Hagar and Ishmael. The cause of the conflict is that

Ishmael mocks his younger brother Isaac at a time when the family are celebrating his birth and growth (Genesis 21:9). Sarah foresees a future problem: Ishmael may take some of her son Isaac's inheritance, and she does not want that to happen. This time she persuades Abraham to drive them away, and he agrees, although not readily. Abraham is distressed as his son going away, and cries out to the Lord, who reassures him that he will provide for them.

So Abraham gives Hagar provision of food and water, and sends them on their way. Inevitably, the water runs out, and Hagar, with no idea what else to do, abandons Ishmael in the desert to die. She goes a short distance away and sobs her heart out, while nearby Ishmael cries out in hunger. The Lord hears these cries and answers them, showing Hagar a well that will provide for their needs. The Lord has decided that since Ishmael is also a son of Abraham, he too will become a great nation. Ishmael lives in the desert, growing up to be an archer, a warrior who, as the angel foretold, was a man of conflict, not of peace.

The Islamic account has both similarities and differences. Although Hajar is not mentioned by name in the Quran, her presence can be inferred from several references, and there are some *ahadith* (sayings) of the Prophet Mohammad that mention her. The basic story of how Ishmael was born in the same in Islam as in the Bible. Sarah cannot conceive, so Ibrahim (as he is named in the Qur'an) has intercourse with Hajar, and she becomes pregnant. Sarah becomes jealous, and asks Ibrahim to send her away. Allah reveals to Ibrahim that he should take Hajar and Ishmael to Makkah, which he duly does. There is great significance in this choice for subsequent Islamic practise, because it was Ibrahim and Ishmael who built the Ka'bah at Makkah (Q 2:124-125), the house that was filled with idols by future generations, and subsequently cleansed by the Prophet Mohammed. But all that was in the future.

17

At present, Hajar was left in the desert, and it was not long before both mother and son suffered immense thirst. As any mother would be, Hajar was more concerned about Ishmael than herself. Desperate to find him something to drink, Hajar ran between the Al-Safa and Al-Marwah hills in search of water for her son. After the seventh run between the two hills, an angel appeared before her. He helped her and told her that God had heard Ishmael's crying and would provide them with water. At that point, God caused a spring to burst forth from the ground, where Ishmael's heel lay, and thereafter Makkah became known for its excellent and abundance of water. The well was subsequently named Zamzam, and become a holy source of water (*ahadith;* see also Q 14:37).

This miracle is commemorated in the hajj (pilgrimage) to Makkah. Part of the pilgrimage is to run seven times between the hills, in commemoration of Hajar's courage and to symbolize the celebration of motherhood in Islam as well as the leadership of women. To complete the task, some Muslims also drink from the Zamzam Well and take some of the water back home from pilgrimage. Hajar is therefore a revered and holy woman within Islam.

There are three differences between these two accounts, one arguably more significant than the others. The minor differences are whether Ishmael was born when Hagar was in the desert, and whether Hagar was taken away by Abraham or fled alone to escape Sarah. Regarding the first difference, in the Islamic account he was already a young boy, while in the account in Genesis he was not yet born the first time Hagar fled, but was on the final expulsion into the desert. This is a difference, but not a significant one. On the second point, the Islamic account associates Ishmael more closely with Abraham than the Genesis one does. This is understandable, given the relative significance of Ishmael to the different faiths. But the most major difference is the significance of Abraham's sons. In Christianity (and Judaism), Isaac is the son of the promise, but in Islam it is Ishmael. It is this difference that is the focus of the study. The conflict here is over identity, specifically the identity of the son whom God chose to be the means through which he brought the promise of blessing to the nations. Muslims, Christians and Jews are all children of Abraham, and can all claim this blessing, but their understanding of the status of their siblings in faith is the source of conflict and disagreement. The story of the almost sacrifice of a son further illustrates the point.

There is also an account of the almost sacrifice of one of Ibrahim's sons in the Quran, but it is Ishmael, not Isaac who is the chosen one. The story differs somewhat from the account in Genesis. Ibrahim has a dream that he will offer his son Ishmael. He tells him of the dream, and Ishmael consents, telling his father to do as he has been commanded. Once they have both submitted to Allah's will, then Allah calls from heaven telling him to spare his son, and providing a great sacrifice in Ishmael's place (Q 37:101-111). The central theme of submission to God is common to both accounts, but the role of the child differs between the Biblical and Quranic accounts. Ishmael is much more of a willing participant that Isaac who, although he does not resist, is ignorant of the divine plan.

This is a further example of the differing understandings of Abraham and his children in the three faiths which all claim descent from him. I do not want to get into that particular debate in any more detail, but rather to suggest a few guiding principles for any disagreement.

First, it is important to remember that we tend to disagree more with those who are close to us than those with whom we have no contact or relationship. To give an example from sport, it is normally the local derby that arouses the greatest passion amongst committed fans. Love and hatred can be closely intertwined; hatred inspires a response, whilst apathy kills everything.

Second, because strong feelings are aroused, it is important to be a good listener and also a good speaker. A good listener gives time and space for the other to express thoughts, feelings and emotions, does not rush in quickly with solutions or advice, and does not allow their own agenda to dominate the conversation. In this context, a good speaker does not exaggerate, blame unnecessarily or use overly emotive or inflammatory language. She speaks about how specific actions have given rise to particular feelings, not to blame, but to facilitate open and honest conversation.

Third, dealing with difficult issues takes courage, time and hard work. It requires courage to become vulnerable, to take the risk of speaking out, of engaging with other people with whom you disagree. It takes time to understand their viewpoint, and to begin to accept differences and begin to construct common ground. As well as time, this building of shared space takes hard work. It is emotionally, spiritually and even physically exhausting to work at overcoming differences. It is far easier to throw rocks from a distance than to take the risk of engagement.

I mentioned that within many sports, it is normally the local derby that arouses the greatest passion. A few examples will illustrate the point. When I lived in Liverpool, I would sometimes visit a family to arrange a funeral for an elderly relative, and be told that the couple had a mixed marriage. This was not a reference to race or religion, but to football. One had been an Evertonian, and the other a Liverpool supporter. The town where I grew up, Cardiff, was known for fierce rivalry with Swansea in football, and any Welsh rugby fan would normally say they supported two teams: Wales, and whoever was playing England at the time. A common understanding and passion for sport, but a clear difference of opinion about who was the best team. This is true of so much more than sport: the Macedonians and the Greeks dispute which country can claim Alexander the Great as their national hero. The Greeks do not accept that Macedonia should really be a separate country, and they certainly do not think as great a historical figure as Alexander could have association with such upstarts. The Macedonians, for their part, are clear that he was a Macedonian, that their country has its own identity, and he is an important figure within their history. One man in history, but two ways of understanding him.

The list of examples could go on. But the main points remain important: we must speak and listen carefully and honestly; understand different viewpoints, and work to establish common ground. It is only from there that we can build a future where conflict is constructive, not destructive. We may disagree in our understanding of history, but hopefully we can still build a future together.

This is an important principle for facing any conflict, namely the ability to listen to each other. People may things we find uncomfortable or disagreeable, but until we have built a bridge of understanding our different viewpoints from the foundation of careful listening, the conflict will never be resolved.

Story

'I'm not eating any of that foreign muck. No way.'

'Sorry, I didn't realise that you only ate authentically English food. Does that mean we should make sure your children don't get any potatoes either?'

'What do you mean?' Frank was confused now, which made me smile inwardly. There was no way I was going to let him see that I was secretly slightly enjoying rattling him.

'Well,' I explained, 'Potatoes aren't actually English are they? Not a native food at all. They originate from the Andes – South America—and the Spanish were the first people to bring them to Europe.'

'Oh, that reminds me of a joke. Where do you find "the Andes"? Frank dodged the point entirely.

'On the end of the armies.' I supplied. 'But, yes, there will be food you'll be happy to eat.'

Organising a bring and share meal to get some of the different groups in our community together was going to be harder work than I'd first thought. We're a very diverse primary school, over 30 nationalities present, and around two hundred children in all. The international food event was an experiment, which would probably work, but which was proving a bit of a pain to organise.

The idea was fairly straightforward. Everyone likes to eat. Most people like their local specialties, and they also like making other people try them. Food makes for common ground, foundations from which to build bridges of some sort of mutual understanding and respect. So far we had a grudging tolerance of difference, a sort of uneasy truce that was all-too-easily broken when some child said something stupid to another.

Take, for example, the time when Amjad had insisted all Muslim girls had to wear a headscarf to be properly Muslim, and began making this point quite loudly to some of the girls in year three whose parents did not think they needed to wear one yet. They may have only been aged eight, but four of them were more than capable of shoving this loud-mouthed ten year old to the ground and kicking him a few times. All in the spirit of mutual understanding between Muslims, of course.

Maybe, I had thought, just maybe, sharing a bit of food together might begin to create an atmosphere were parents could talk to each other a bit more freely, in school coffee mornings and so on. What I had not thought about was the nerves and uncertainty that the simple idea of getting together would generate. I am used to meeting all kinds of people, and getting on with people who are nothing like me.

But most of our parents are not. To put it mildly. Many of them struggle to get on with their own families, never mind people of a different race or religion. Hence Frank's concern about what he would have to eat.

Fortunately he was persuaded that he would not have to eat 'foreign muck' (by which I think he meant curries of a type he did not recognise as being English by virtue of being served at the local chippie). Frank was not the first, or the last, parent to express concerns about exactly what would happen at the international food event. Several parents wanted to know if they could charge for the food there were making, because 'meat is expensive. And the spices are not cheap either.' Some wondered how they would know which dish was halal. Others expressed variants on the theme of suspicion of anything unusual, including two parents who explained why mashed potatoes were an abomination.

Happily, the event itself did sort itself. People brought food, far too much food, and had a great time eating far too much. Most people stuck within their comfort zones, venturing to the edges and trying dishes that looked a bit like things they were more familiar with. A few brave souls tried some of the extra spicy curry that had been made specially, and spent the rest of the afternoon drinking gallons of water, and then having to make frequent trips to the bathroom, as the water worked its way inevitably downwards. We did make a start, a small one, at establishing some sort of community. At least, the next few coffee mornings were slightly more civil. It has always struck me that one of the most important parts of establishing community is shared positive experience, and what better way of doing that than over a shared meal?

Questions for discussion

I used to be chair of governors for a primary school that had a regular international food event, and it was not at all a stressful experience, although the clearing up at the end was sometimes quite hard work! I have spent the last seven years living in multi-cultural inner city areas, and while I have always found them to be fantastic places to live, I know that some people find it very hard to live so close to people who are very different from them. I can imagine that for some people, even something as simple as sharing food across cultures may in fact be quite a nerve-wracking experience.

In discussing the different accounts of Sarah and Hagar and their sons, I wanted to try and make clear how stark those differences sometimes are. There is a lot of common ground in the two accounts, but also a lot to disagree about, perhaps very passionately. When things are very personal, ideas that we hold close to our hearts, it is difficult to avoid getting emotionally involved and so we end up saying things in a way we do not quite mean, or even deliberately trying to hurt other people as a way of defending ourselves.

1. What is your experience of spending time with people who are very different from you? How easy do you find it to do?

2. What did you think of the different accounts of Hagar/Hajar and the different views about Isaac and Ishmael?

3. Can you think of examples of things that people who live near you disagree about passionately?

    Read Genesis 16. We're now thinking about the story entirely from the perspective of the Genesis account.

1. In what ways did Abram act wrongly in having a son by Hagar? Whose fault do you think this was?

2. How might Abram have acted differently?

3. What do we learn about God from how he cares for Hagar and Ishmael? What does that teach us about how we should disagree with other people?

Isaac gets married

It is all very well to talk about keeping yourself pure and uncorrupted by the world, but what does that actually mean in practise? It is all very well to say you are following God's will for your life, but how do you know that is what you are doing? How can you be sure you are following God's will, and not in fact living a lie? These are the areas I would like to explore in this chapter. I will use the story of Isaac's marriage as a means of discussing the conflict between purity and pollution, and the challenge of discerning God's guidance as I think they are closely related to each other, and they both lie at the heart of the normal Christian life.

The story of Isaac's marriage is found in Genesis 24. Abraham is old. Very old, given he was already one hundred when Isaac was born and now the time has come for Isaac to be married. Abraham is worried about the purity of his family line. Purity in terms of ethnicity and also purity in terms of faith. The Canaanites who surround him cannot provide a suitable wife, so he looks back to his own people for an appropriate spouse for Isaac. Abraham himself is too ancient to make the long journey to find someone, so he entrusts the task to one of his servants. It is such an important task that he does not just pick any servant, but his senior servant, the man in charge of his whole household. This man is asked to swear a solemn oath, to commit himself to fulfilling the task that Abraham now gives him.

The difficulty is not in finding an eligible woman, but an appropriate one, for she must be prepared to travel to Isaac, as he cannot come to her. Abraham believes the only way for the Lord's promise to him will be fulfilled will be if his family stays where he has been called. This means Isaac must remain in Canaan and his wife should come to him. Abraham is sure that just as the Lord has preserved Isaac so far, he will continue to honour his promise and give Isaac descendants who can live in the land of Canaan, fulfilling the expectation that Abraham's descendants would inherit the land (Genesis 24:5-9).

So the servant departs, and travels to find Isaac a wife. He has no idea who to ask, so he hands responsibility for selection to the Lord, simply asking that when he needs water, it be offered by the chosen woman to both him and his camels. Faced with an impossible task, of knowing whom to ask, this seems like a sensible choice; entrusting God to guide is not leaving it to chance, but acknowledging that he is sovereign over the course of all of human history. And that is exactly how it turned out. Rebekah comes to draw water, and offers it to both the servant and enough to satisfy his camels. The servant goes with her to her brother and father, recounts his mission, the way he tested it out, and Rebekah's unknowing completion of the task he had set her. They are pleased to accept the dowry offered for Rebekah's hand. She herself is willing to go where she is asked, and duly goes with the servant, marries Isaac and comforts him after his mother's death (Genesis 24:10-67).

Although this is not the way marriage partners are selected in Britain today, and indeed we may find the method of selecting a bride unconventional or uncomfortable, nevertheless the process does seem quite straightforward and uncontested. We also have to remember the particular purpose this marriage plays in the plans and purposes of God: it was essential for Isaac's family to remain faithful to the covenant Abraham made with God, and Isaac's wife would be central to that, as she would be the one who brought up Isaac's heir. There are two inter-linked questions at the heart of this story:

how will Isaac's family remain pure and how will they know that God has guided them to the right wife for Isaac?

I'd like to think about the question of purity first. Abraham rightly recognised that if Isaac married a Canaanite, he would have been very unlikely to remain faithful to Yahweh. He also knew he had been promised an inheritance in the land of Canaan, and so was not prepared for Isaac to leave that land to find a wife. This dilemma perfectly illustrates the challenge of being in but not of the world. There is a constant conflict which all Christians face, that of being connected to but not consumed by the culture which surrounds them. The details differ from the dilemma which Abraham faced, but the central conflict remains the same.

The whole story of the people of God is a story of this conflict between purity and pollution. Generations later, when the people leave Egypt and eventually re-enter the Promised Land, they are warned about the danger of pollution, of becoming too like the inhabitants of Canaan. Sadly they do not heed those warnings, and the book of Judges records how quickly the people turned away from following God's way. Time and again he raised up a new leader, a new judge to rescue them from peril, but each time the cycle of repentance followed by rescue followed by a return to sin and falling away followed by punishment and suffering leading to repentance, just got worse, and became a downward spiral, until right at the end of the book of Judges, we end up with boasting womanisers like Samson being called as God's rescuers. The very closing line of the book: 'in those days Israel had no king; everyone did as they saw fit' (Judges 21:25) tells us the author's opinion of the situation. Without a king to guide them, to steer them towards purity and away from pollution by the world, the people of God have a tendency to curve in on themselves, to be distracted and drawn into disobedience. Being pure is hard work; living a polluted life is less effort, but much more destructive.

Sadly, once the people of Israel do have a king, they do not fare much better. One of the refrains throughout the history

27

of the kings of Israel in particular is that they fail to destroy the 'high places,' the hill-top shrines that were dedicated to the Canaanite fertility cults. These prove to be a real source of pollution at the heart of Israelite faith, drawing people away from the purity of worshipping Yahweh. The problem is compounded by the fact that after the first two kings, David and Solomon, the kingdom splits in two, and there are two rival places of worship: in Jerusalem and in Samaria. The pollution of greed and ambition begins to eat away at the purity of faith.

This description of pollution throughout the history of the people of God could go on and on and one. It is a constant battle: Jesus prayed for his disciples, not that they would be taken out of the world, even though they did not belong there, but that they would be saved from the pollution of the evil one, the devil (John 17:15-16). We all have to work hard at maintaining a disciplined Christian life, not living as though our own efforts will save us, but doing our best to live in a way that will please God.

Part of the problem, of course, is that we are not always quite sure exactly what it is that God wants us to do. Let us return to Abraham's servant, facing the task of finding a wife for Isaac. How was he supposed to know whom to approach? He had travelled to approximately the right location, so far, so good. But that was, although dangerous and arduous, the relatively easy part. The far harder task was finding the right person. Whom should it be?

The question of guidance is a difficult one, and I will not be able to solve all the issues in this short discussion. What I would like to point out is that, in faith, Abraham's servant set a relatively straightforward test, and used it to discern the Lord's will. The test is simple but also sophisticated. The servant was, I think, looking for a servant-hearted wife for Isaac, someone who would care for other's needs, and not just human needs, but someone who recognised the importance of animals, vital for the livelihood of travelling nomads, such as Abraham and Isaac. The test was, will she offer me water and my camels water? Will she care for human beings and for animals? If she does, then she will be the one.

You may be thinking that is no way to select a wife, but ask yourself is it really any more arbitrary that simply waiting for a chance meeting and feeling right about it? I think there was probably more to it in Isaac's day, just as there is more to it in our day, but the crucial point is that God was sovereign, and God guided Abraham's servant to the woman he had chosen.

There are many other stories in the Bible of people setting slightly arbitrary tests to check they know what God wants them to do. I'll give just two examples. Think of the story of Gideon: a coward whom God chose to rescue Israel. He had two tests for the Lord: first he wanted a wool fleece to be wet and the surrounding ground dry, and then he wanted the reverse to be the case: the fleece dry and the ground wet (Judges 6). Second, at a much later point in the history of the people of God, they want to choose a new apostle to replace Judas Iscariot. They have a discussion about suitable candidates and then draw lots to decide which of the chosen two should be selected (Acts 1:12-26). God works in and through history, and so it should not surprise us that he uses the circumstances of history to shape the pattern of history.

This does not solve the problem of guidance, but it might give us a few ideas: often we can rely on common sense in working out what God's will is, although the example of Gideon should remind us that the Lord is not always sensible as we might understand common sense. We can also rely on the advice of other Christians: this is perhaps especially helpful if we feel we're being called to do something that does not seem completely sensible by conventional standards. We can certainly rely on the Bible: if we think we're being called to do something that is against the clear teaching of Scripture, then we are wrong. Familiarity with the Bible may also help deal with the issue of common sense: from the Lord's perspective being generous to the poor, refusing to be join in with the gossip or backstabbing to get a promotion at work are all completely sensible, even if the conventional wisdom of society might say otherwise. In these circumstances, it is the compelling Spirit, the voice of the God who lives inside us, that helps us see what we are supposed to do. The Spirit takes the word of God, and applies it to our lives, helping us know how we are supposed to live.

Guidance and purity seem to me to go hand-in-glove: if we know exactly what it is God wants us to do, then we will be better able to keep ourselves pure. Our circumstances may give us some hints, common sense may point us in certain directions, our fellow believers should be able to help direct us, and most of all our familiarity with the Bible and our ability to listen to God's Spirit should help keep us at least walking in roughly the right direction.

Perhaps a prayer by Thomas Merton will helps us as we struggle with purity and guidance:

> My Lord God, I have no idea where I am going. I do not see the road ahead of me. I cannot know for certain where it will end nor do I really know myself, and the fact that I think that I am following your will does not mean that I am actually doing so. But I believe that the desire to please you does in fact please you. And I hope I have that desire in all that I am doing. I hope that I will never do anything apart from that desire. And I know that if I do this you will lead me by the right road though I may know nothing about it. Therefore will I trust you always though I may seem to be lost and in the shadow of death. I will not fear, for you are ever with me, and you will never leave me to face my perils alone.

Story

'I have to tell you, I think anyone who says they hear God talk to them in an audible way probably is a fruitcake of the nuttiest variety and should be sectioned,' Jenny said, with a little smile, but also a slight air of despair. 'I just do not know what it is that I am supposed to do about this.'

'Do you want to talk about it?' Natasha asked, taking a sip of her hot chocolate. 'I'm not in a hurry. It's Saturday morning, yeah, I want to do some shopping at some point today, but there's no rush at all. Saturday mornings are made for this sort of a conversation.'

'You sure?' checked Jenny. 'It'll take a while.'

'No problem.' Natasha stretched her legs, took another sip to fortify herself for listening, and waved a welcoming gesture. 'The floor is yours, begin at the beginning.'

'Oh, good grief, where do I begin?' Jenny sipped her latte while she thought.

Natasha just waited quietly, taking a bite from her almond croissant, and glancing at the shoppers walking purposefully past the coffee shop window as Jenny collected her thoughts. They'd been friends for several years, and these Saturday morning meetings were a regular part of their week, an important opportunity to ask for advice, share gossip and enjoy relaxing in each other's company.

'You know I want this promotion at work,' Jenny began abruptly. A secondary school history teacher, Jenny had been considering applying for the role of head of department for about eighteen months, and the topic had come up on more than one Saturday morning.

'Yeah, I know.' Natasha confirmed.

'Well, our current head of department announced this week that he's leaving. I had no idea, but he'd applied for an assistant head's post at the new academy, and got it. I've no idea how, as the man is a fool.'

'You've said.' Natasha interjected, keen to steer the conversation away from another rant about the incompetence of Jenny's immediate boss, a man whose failings she was already well aware of, having been briefed by Jenny on more than one Saturday morning.

'Like I've said, an idiot. So that's the problem.' Jenny explained, taking another sip.

'Sorry, what is?' Natasha was confused, and her puzzled expression must have shown that to Jenny.

'Do I want to apply for the job of replacing an idiot? The department is a mess, and if we get inspected this year—as we probably will—then it will look as though the mess is my fault.'

'Oh, I see. But surely you can come up with a plan to sort things out, and however far you get, that's how far you've got?'

'But I'm not sure Ofsted are that kind,' Jenny clarified. 'And there's several other people in the department who might apply. And I'm the only Christian really. I sometimes get a bit of flack for that, and I don't want to make it worse by suddenly being everyone's boss.'

'Let me see if I've got this right?' Natasha had put her drink down, and was looking straight at Jenny. She ticked the points off on her fingers as she summarised, 'First there's the issue of the department being a mess.'

'Yep.'

'Second, there's the question of an Ofsted, and who will be blamed for the mess.'

'That's a killer, that is, and..'

'Hang on, can I finish summarising?'

'Oh, yeah, go on, this is really helpful.'

'Okay,' said Natasha, with her gaze still fully on Jenny. 'Third, there's the question of you being the only Christian, and whether being head of department will make that harder for you?'

'Well, not just harder for me, also whether it will be a bad witness if I get the blame for the mess the department's in.'

'Oh, okay, sorry, so third, the issue of Christian witness and the other two things I've already mentioned?'

'That's it. So what should I do?' Jenny asked, passing her problem neatly to Natasha, and taking another sip of her latte as she waited for the solution.

'I'm not sure I can tell you that,' Natasha countered. 'But I'm happy to keep talking about what you think you should do. Is that okay?'

'Sure.'

'Well,' said Natasha, 'Let's look at them in order. Problem one: things are a mess. You're good at sorting out messes, and you like doing it, and you're capable of sorting this one. That's right?'

'Yeah, I guess. I do like tidying stuff up, and yeah, I do think I could get the department into a much better shape than it is at the moment.' Jenny sat up a bit straighter, pushing her shoulders back, head held high, pushing back the sleeves of her jumper as if she was ready to begin at that very moment.

'Calm down, you can't start yet.' Natasha smiled. 'Have you got a plan for what you'd do, and can you explain it well?'

'I think so.' Jenny said, tilting her head to one side as she considered. 'Yeah, I think I could.'

'Great,' Natasha affirmed. 'So you could do it, given enough time. That answers question one. Now to the issue of Ofsted. When might you be inspected?'

'No idea,' Jenny shrugged. 'We're due one. We were "good" under the old framework. We won't be that under the new one. There would need to be a lot of work done.'

'But if you can come up with a plan that shows what you're doing, then that's the best you can do isn't it?'

'Well, I think it is,' said Jenny, preparing to mount another favourite soapbox. 'But the thing about Ofsted is...'

'Yeah, they're idiots. You've told me.' Natasha deftly interjected. 'Let's stick with you and this job application for the moment, okay?'

'Alright.' Jenny climbed back down from her soapbox. 'So you're saying you think if I have a plan that documents what I want to do, even if I get inspected straight after taking over, then I won't get all the blame?'

'Yeah, I don't see how you could. You just need to make sure you've got a plan written down, and you're able to demonstrate you're acting on it. At least, that's what it seems to me.'

'You're probably right.' Jenny took another sip of her coffee.

'Okay, so the last question is the one about being a Christian, and whether it's a bad witness. Can you explain that one to me a bit more, as I don't really think I understood what you meant.'

'Well,' said Jenny, leaning forward. 'Its like this. Most of the department aren't Christians, and to be honest, they seem to think Christians are a bit stupid. I wouldn't want to get the job, get a bad report, and confirm their prejudices. Do you see what I mean?'

'So what you're saying is, you think if you get the job and if you get a bad report, then people in your department will think all Christians are idiots, and simply because of this one bad report won't convert to Christianity. Have I got that right?'

'Now you put it like that, I'm not sure I do think that.' Jenny leant back in her seat, looked up at the ceiling and considered it again. 'I guess that's make a bit of a mountain out of a molehill, isn't it?'

'Could be,' said Natasha, in as non-committal a voice as she could manage.

'Yeah, it is, I know what you're doing.' Jenny smiled. 'You're reflecting back to me what I've been saying to help me see where I'm being sensible and where I'm being silly aren't you? I remember that course you talked about.'

'Could be,' said Natasha, in the same neutral voice, but with a twinkle in her eyes.

'Could be. Whatever. You are. And its helpful, thanks. Now I hear it like that, there really isn't a reason to not apply is there?'

'Well, I can't see one,' smiled Natasha. 'Yeah, I was practising my reflective listening skills, and they seem to have worked okay on you. So what do you think?'

'Yeah, I will apply. And I will write out a plan of action. And Ofsted can do take a running jump if they do come. Do you want another drink? My treat.'

'Yeah, hot chocolate again please?'

'Coming right up.'

Questions for discussion

In the story that came after the Bible reflection, I concentrated on the issue of guidance, and specifically on helping someone else work out what they should do in a particular situation. I have tried to give an example of a process called 'reflective listening.' Essentially, it is a way of helping someone hear their own thoughts and so come to a clearer understanding of what they themselves think about a particular situation.

The most important part of reflective listening is that the listener does not offer their own opinion unless they are directly asked to do so by the person speaking. Instead you simply summarise and reflect back what it is you hear. This should be done in as neutral a manner as possible, not offering any judgement on what you have heard, but rather giving the speaker an opportunity to hear for themselves what they are saying, and so arrive at a more considered opinion.

When we are trying to decide how to make a difficult decision, it is important that we know clearly what we think, and the purpose of reflective listening is to help someone arrive at that clarity. It may feel unnatural at first, as our instinct is often to leap in with an opinion or advice, but once you get used to it, you will discover that reflective listening is a powerful tool to help others recognise what they think and so make much better decisions.

1. Have you ever experienced reflective listening, either as the person listening or as the person being listened to? What was it like?

2. Why do you think it is so important that anyone facing conflict is listened to?

3. What ways do you think help people receive guidance from God?

Read Genesis 24

1. What can we learn from the attitude of Abraham's servant in relation to his master and the task given to him?

2. What can we learn from the way the servant made his choice?

3. What picture do we get of Rebekah?

36

Isaac's conflict over water

'Ok, you cut. I'll choose.'

'Why do I have to cut?'

'Because I'm older and I say so, that's why.'

'Well I'm going to get a ruler first.'

'Fine, whatever. I'm still choosing first. And if you use a ruler to measure to cut, then I'm using it to choose.'

At the heart of many conflicts is the problem of scarce resources. In the fictional (but probably easily recognisable) conversation above, it was that age-old problem of two siblings both wanting half of the final piece of cake. It was not a dispute about cake, but conflict over scarce resources was part of Isaac's experience. In his case it was over water and land. Like his father, Abraham, Isaac was a pastoral nomad. He travelled with his animals, and this meant there was not always enough for them to eat or drink. As his wealth increased, he ended up travelling to find new territory that was able to provide for his needs.

Genesis 26 recounts how Isaac lived first with Abimelech of the Philistines, then in the Gerar valley, then he moved on again from there, before settling finally in Beersheba. Each time his herdsmen dug new wells and each time there was a conflict over access to water. In a dry and thirsty land access to water meant access to life, so it is hardly surprising that this was the source of the conflict.

It begins when Isaac is in Gerar, the land of the Philistines. Isaac stays there because that is where the Lord tells him he should be. There was a famine, so the tempting solution would have been to travel to Egypt, where life would have been easier. But the Lord did not want Isaac to do that: he was to stay in the land he had been promised, and the Lord would provide for him, proving the reliability of his word and the greatness of his power (Genesis 26:1-6).

The first problem Isaac faces is what to say about his wife, Rebekah. She is beautiful, he is afraid of being killed so someone else can marry her, and so he resorts to a lie of his father's, telling Abimelek, king of the Philistines, that Rebekah is just his sister. He is soon caught out in that lie, and has to admit the truth. It may seem crude to put it this way, but beautiful women are also a limited resource, and Isaac's response to the potential threat to himself and his wife is to lie, not trust in the Lord. But he soon learnt his lesson: God had promised the land to Isaac and his descendants, and so of course that meant he protected both Isaac and Rebekah. This is an important lesson for us to learn: the Lord promises to provide, and he does, but we have to learn to trust in his provision (Genesis 26:7-11).

The main focus of my discussion here is the on-going conflict over the scarce resource of water. The Philistines had stopped up the wells that Abraham had dug, but Isaac re-digs them, because he has so many animals, and needs so much water. This becomes the well *Esek* or 'Contention,' because the local herdsmen claim it as their own. Isaac is gracious and moves on, digging another well. But the problem does not end. The next well is *Sitnah* or 'Enmity,' as the controversy over access to water continues. Isaac moves on again, and finally is able to dig a well which is not a source of controversy, so it is named *Rehoboth*, or 'Room,' because finally they have room in the land to flourish (Genesis 26:12-22).

There is a challenging principle for us in the conflict over scarce resources: sometimes we have to keep moving until we come to the place of the Lord's provision for us. There is enough resource available in the world for everyone to flourish, but that may mean we cannot stay exactly where we would like, doing exactly what we want. Sometimes we have to move to the place where the Lord will provide for us.

From the well *Rehoboth* Isaac goes to Beer-Sheba, where the Lord appears to him, to reassure him and comfort him. And Isaac's servants dig another well. He at last makes peace with Abimelech, king of the Philistines, so the final well is named *Shibah*, or 'Oath,' commemorating the oath of peace made between them. It takes a long time, and some considerable sacrifice before Isaac has uncontested resources sufficient to provide for his needs. What is important for us to note is his willingness to surrender what could be argued to be rightfully his, in order to keep the peace with his neighbours (Genesis 26:23-33).

There is a long history of sharing of scarce resources in the Bible. I'll give three examples. The first comes when the people of God are in the desert, having left Egypt. The Lord provides food for them: quail and manna from heaven. Everyone is expected to gather enough to meet their own needs but not too much. If they are greedy, and take more than they need, then it goes off, except when they gather two days provisions so they will not have to work on the Sabbath (Exodus 16). The Apostle Paul uses this piece of history when he writes to the church in Corinth, encouraging them to give financially to support the needy church in Jerusalem. The principle is not of taking more than be afforded, but of equality, so that everyone has what they need to survive (2 Corinthians 8-9). Finally, the early church ended up in a conflict over the distribution of scarce resources to provide for widows in need; the apostles appointed deacons to oversee the distribution of aid to the poor, again to ensure everyone had enough and that no one had too much or too little (Acts 6:1-7).

I remember taking a religious education lesson for a reception class, children aged four and five. We talked about the importance of sharing, about how this was a way of showing your classmates that you cared for them. The children were really good at giving me examples of sharing. The problem was that five minutes later, when the lesson was over and they were enjoying free play, quite a few of them were squabbling over toys, struggling to share with each other. The conflict here was over the scarce resource of toys. They could talk the theory of sharing, but the practice of sharing was far harder.

While we may all smile at this example, the fact is, many of us behave just like that, because we always want more than our fair share of the planet's resources. The toddler rules of ownership are quite apt descriptions of the conflict over possessions many of us get embroiled in. They go something like this

1. If I want it, it's mine;

2. If it's in my hand, it's mine;

3. If I can take it away from you, it's mine;

4. If I had it a little while ago, it's mine;

5. If it's mine, it must never appear to be yours in any way;

6. If we are building something together, all the pieces are mine;

7. If it just looks like mine, it's mine;

8. If I think it's mine, it's mine;

9. If I give it to you and change my mind later, it's mine;

10. If it is broken, it's all yours.

Although we may not want to admit it, we may find ourselves unconsciously operating by a similar set of rules. We're probably not as blunt as toddlers, but is that just because we've got better at hiding our true feelings rather than because we've truly learnt how to share?

The question of conflict over scarce resources can be examined on many different levels. I will comment briefly on four: international; national; local and personal. On an international level there is both an awful lot we can do and nothing we can do. There is nothing we can do in the sense that although we all participate in global inequality, we feel powerless to change things. How can one person lift millions out of the poverty imposed on them by unfair trade agreements, debts their rulers from a generation or more ago signed up to and so on? What difference can I make to a world that is unjust, where the rich are getting richer and the poor are getting poorer?

Perhaps not that much. But we must recognise where we stand. Like me, you are probably on the side of the unequally wealthy. As a vicar, with a house provided with my job, a wife who is a full time mum and one pre-school child, I am in the richest 12% of the world's population. (To see where you fit, visit `http://www.givingwhatwecan.org/why-give/how-rich-am-i`, and take their simple on-line test.) So although as a family we do struggle with the rising cost of living, and money is tight for us, I have to recognise that it is a lot tighter for most of the world's population. Moreover, I have to recognise that I can make a difference. Buying fairtrade is one example; another might be thinking about how much I consume, asking myself, 'do I need this, or do I just want it?' when I am thinking about buying something. We can campaign politically: the more of us who join our voices to campaigns about global inequality, the more impact they will have. Our individual efforts may only be a tiny pebble against a mountain of injustice, but pile up enough pebbles and you will eventually draw level to the mountain peak.

While we are only able to do so much internationally, there are certainly things we can do nationally and locally. Consumers are becoming increasingly concerned about where their shopping comes from, and initiatives such as the Bristol pound, a currency only for use in certain shops in Bristol by people who live in Bristol is just one example of how people are trying to support local businesses. It is much easier to be aware of, and to campaign about, local rather than international, or even nation issues.

Most importantly, what do we do about the scarce resources of our own home and family? On a personal level, are we generous with what we have, or are we always trying to get more for ourselves? I think it is only when we get our own house in order that we can start to begin to play our part in dealing with the more complex national and international issues.

When God made the world, he put human beings in charge, as stewards of creation. The planet's resources are finite, so it is up to us to ensure they are put to their best possible use. There is more than enough in our world for everyone to have everything they need, even if there is not enough for everyone to have everything they want.

So the challenge that Isaac's wells give each one of us is: how do we respond to conflict over scarce resources? Sharing is difficult because it involves recognising that others have a right to use—or even keep—things we think of as our own. But when we learn to see things from God's perspective, then, in theory at least, sharing should get easier. The reality is that everything we have is a gift of God; it is all his, and we are merely stewards responsible for taking care of it for a while. Jesus reminds us, in the parable of the talents, that God expects those who have been given much to use their wealth responsibly (Matthew 25:14-30). When he is encouraging the Christians in Corinth to give, Paul reminds them of all they have received from the Lord Jesus (2 Corinthians 8:9). Thus the question remains: the Lord has been very generous to us. How generous can we be to others in response?

Story

The cupboard was clearly marked. 'TODDLERS GROUP ONLY.' Inside there was a cheap jar of instant coffee, an opened packet of teabags, a half-full bag of sugar, a few teaspoons and a pack of the cheapest custard creams you have ever had the misfortune to eat. Not that you would have been able to discover this, as the cupboard itself was locked shut, with a padlock so huge it would have been better placed keeping a large wrought iron gate closed in a prison.

I looked at that notice again, and sighed. It was an amazingly difficult conversation to have, the discussion about those cupboards. The toddlers group had one, the ladies group had one, the lunch club had one, the Sunday school had one, the music group had one, the Bible study group had one and the mothers' union had two (a source of indignation to everyone else). Many of the same people went to several of these groups, and the same lady even ran the mid-week Bible study and lunch club. But each group had their own cupboard, with its own lock, and its own separate supply of cheap refreshments. There were separate refreshments for use on a Sunday as well, and these were not locked up, as in everyone's view was that this tea and coffee should be available to everyone, even if none of the groups ever actually used it.

I can still remember the meeting in which I had the audacity to suggest that maybe having all these separate supplies of tea and coffee was a bit silly, and a bit of a waste of space. I still remember the meeting because I still remember being told off in no uncertain terms by so many people. I had, apparently, completely failed to understand the seriousness of the situation. 'Some people' (unspecified) had been helping themselves to 'other people's' supplies without asking, and without replacing them. This had led to several 'near disasters' and 'very serious situations' where groups had started 'up to ten minutes late' and people had to 'rush out and buy extra supplies from the local shop, which is much more expensive,' and moreover, 'run by a very unsavoury gentleman.'

Idiot that I am, I had pressed on, asking why the church could not simply bulk buy fair trade tea and coffee, and make that freely available to everyone. I could not have been more stupid. While the concept of fair trade was grudgingly supported by several individuals, the idea of paying more than was absolutely necessary for church refreshments was a heresy, one so serious that there was the possibility of being burnt at the stake if you suggested it twice.

At some point, even vicars know when to shut up, and with plenty of other business for us to grumble and argue over, I moved the meeting on, resolving to do some more digging into the background issues at a later point in time. Several weeks later, I was having a chat with a churchwarden, and the topic of the cupboards came up. Steve is a friendly, relaxed guy, and I thought that he would perhaps be able to enlighten me as to the strong feelings. Fortunately, I was right.

It turned out that the idiot vicar's idea of having bulk supplies had been tried in the past, but with a crucial flaw in the plan: the tea and coffee were all paid for by one particular individual, who thought it would be a way of being generous to the church. As sometimes happens, this was less about secret giving and more about public generosity to boost personal reputation and standing, a chance to become a bigger fish in a remarkably small pond. Almost innevitably for an attempt to boost personal status through public generosity, the tea and coffee scheme was a dismal failure. The scheme had taken place when fair trade was in its infancy, the idea still novel to most people. The quality of the fair trade instant coffee was viewed by some as 'limited,' to put it politely, and the life-long

Nescafe addicts really did not want to make the switch. One of them took matters into her own hands, staging a guerilla raid on the tin of fair trade granules, substituting the contents for a tin of Nescafe. Sadly her deception was discovered (she had thrown the fairtrade coffee into the kitchen bin one Saturday night, so it was not hard to work out what had happened). No one admitted responsibility, but suspicion was firmly directed at one of three ladies (hence the female pronouns), none of whom had convincingly denied responsibility, and all of whom had been vocal critics of the 'fairtrade foultaste' as they dubbed it.

The benefactor, stung by the insult, resorted to locking fairtrade coffee for one group in a cupboard, and once locks started to be deployed each group slowly followed suit, until eventually every single group had its own locked cupboard, and the available space in the church kitchen was drastically reduced. Since the matter had never been properly dealt with, the problem of fair trade coffee became the symptom of a much deeper conflict within the life of the church, a sign that people were unable to be honest and open with each other.

Once I realised that this was the problem, there was really only one thing that could be done, and that was to make people talk about it. I followed a fairly straightforward strategy, meeting first of all with individuals whom I thought were involved in the issue, in order to clarify whom I really needed to speak to. This took several months of slightly awkward conversations, but I stuck with it, and eventually identified four key individuals whom I thought should join me for a discussion together.

I won't bore you with all the details of what was said, but will simply outline a bit of the process we followed. First everyone was given a chance to express their own opinion on the subject. This was the hardest part, because no one was allowed to interrupt. One at a time, I asked people to express their views, their feelings to the group. Each time I summarised what I thought I had heard, allowed the speaker to clarify what they had meant, and then moved on to the next person. So for example, the original benefactor was able to explain how hurt she had felt when she had seen all that 'expensive coffee wasted,' and that it had felt 'like a real slap in my face, like my generosity was being thrown back at me, and the church was saying they hated me and did not want me there.' Once other people thought of it in those terms, they saw the foolishness of their own actions, and although they still talked about how they 'hated the taste of that fairtrade foultaste,' they also were able to say that, 'perhaps we didn't deal with it in the best possible way.'

Once everyone had a chance to say what they thought, I asked the group what they thought of the situation, and whether they had any possible solutions. Happily someone soon commented that 'it is a bit silly having seven different supplies of tea and coffee locked next to each other.' Maybe, a different person suggested, the best solution would be to have a few available options, including both fairtrade coffee and also a different brand available for those who really did not like the taste. Everyone seemed quite content with this, and happily the church is now able to cope with the challenging issue of sharing tea and coffee. The cupboards have been put to better use, and people seem much happier, about this issue at least. Mind you, the PCC also want to think about redecorating the main church sanctuary, including replacing the carpet, so the meeting to discuss what colour we choose is bound to be real fun...

Questions for discussion

The story above is entirely fictional, but is drawn from twelve years experience in working for churches in a variety of contexts. For some reason, church cupboards are often a source of conflict, normally because no one is entirely sure who is responsible for looking after them, and busy people are not always good at replacing things they have taken. Sometimes, as in this somewhat tongue-in-cheek story, things get a bit more out of hand, and an unresolved hurt leads to an ongoing inability to share. In this scenario, patient and careful listening, the opportunity to express differences and talk about hurts are important. Sometimes apparently trivial or silly disagreements are in fact the surface manifestations of far deeper and more complex problems.

In the story, I briefly outlined one important tool for helping people resolve issues, and that is what I'll call a 'talking circle'. The rules of running the 'talking circle' must be strictly enforced for it to function. There are different ways you can run it, but in this example, each person speaks in turn, and what they have said is summarised and reflected back to them by the person running the circle. In a situation of conflict, such as the one described, this is probably the best approach. Different issues might lend themselves to other approaches, such as having the next speaker summarise what they have heard before speaking themselves.

As I said, this is a made up example, but one I can certainly imagine happening.

1. What do you think of the idea of a 'talking circle'? Can you imagine a situation where it might help resolve a disagreement?

2. Why do you think we find sharing so difficult? How can we help each other as individuals get better at sharing?

3. How can we as a church model good sharing and generosity?

Read Genesis 26

4. Isaac's conflict over water

1. Why do you think Isaac found it so hard to trust God when he was in danger?

2. What changed him?

3. What can we learn from the quarrel over the wells?

Jacob the trickster

Conflict between brothers is common, and Jacob and Esau were no exception to this rule. It was almost as if they simply hated each other from birth, or maybe even before they were born. When she was pregnant, Rebekah became conscious of a jostling within her womb, and she enquired of the Lord about this. He revealed to her that two nations were striving within her, two peoples who have struggled to this day. They were even born struggling; Jacob came out grasping his brother's heel, an act for which he was named. It turned out to be a very apt name. Jacob grew up to be a grasper, a grabber at other people's possessions. It meant there was real tension between him and his brother (Genesis 25:21-26).

Esau, the tall, hairy, rugged outdoors type was his father's favourite, while the quieter, gentler, softer Jacob was his mother's boy. Most likely there was conflict over parental affection, which culminated in Jacob's plot to steal his brother's blessing. Esau had already given Jacob his birthright, his inheritance, in exchange for a meal. Jacob had grasped the better portion from Esau. But this victory was not enough for Jacob. He wanted everything.

The idea originally came from Rebekah, his mother. She heard Isaac's plan to bless Esau, and summoned Jacob to join her scheme to trick Isaac. Wearing goat skin to make himself hairy, carrying food his mother had cooked, Jacob grasped his brother's blessing, snatching from him the one thing his father had left to give.

This final crime really was a crime too far. Jacob knew staying put would most likely result in death. So he ran.

The Lord has a strange way of using our failures to change us, to mould us into the people he wants us to be. Jacob had grasped everything he could from his brother, and now he ran from him. But in his flight he met with God in a number of different ways.

First of all, he encountered God in a dream. He had made it as far as Bethel, a place whose name means 'house of God.' In his dream, Jacob saw the angels ascending and descending to the heavens. The Lord himself appeared to Jacob, revealing his own name and character, and promising guidance and descendants to Jacob. There is an important lesson for anyone who is in conflict here. While we may not be recipients of exactly the same blessings or promises as Jacob, we can recognise that even in the midst of our sinfulness and failure the Lord is at work in our lives. Jacob has begun to change as a result of his dream. He promises to make offerings to God if he is cared for while he travels and makes it safely home. It is a bit of a hollow promise from a trickster, but at least he is beginning to recognise his need of personal surrender to the Lord.

Second, I think Jacob learnt his real lessons about conflict in the episode that followed. The trickster was himself tricked, by his uncle Laban. Jacob ought to have seen it coming. He arrived at his uncle's village, and falls in love with his younger daughter Rachel before he has even met Laban. He agrees to work for Laban for seven years in return for Rachel's hand in marriage.

Seven years is a long time, and you might have thought it was long enough for Jacob to work out that Laban's elder daughter Leah was unmarried and that custom dictated she had to be married first. But Jacob either did not realise or did not care. He just wanted to have sex with Rachel, and was bored of waiting. So he agreed to a wedding celebration, but woke up the next morning beside Leah, not Rachel.

His conflict with his father-in-law began from that moment. Jacob did get to marry Rachel, so from that perspective he got what he wanted. But his own household was filled with conflict as his wives competed for his attention and each sought to bear more children for him, even using their slave girls as part of the competition. Jacob also worked at weakening Laban's livestock and strengthening his own. And when he decided it was time to return home, over fourteen years after he left, Rachel stole her father's household gods, arguably his most precious possessions.

Jacob had learnt something about conflict, but was still caught up in the midst of it. He had made his promise to God, but his first encounter had not been enough to change him for good. In the end, Jacob ends up in physical conflict with God, and it is this bruising encounter that truly changes him. All of us can live in contested situations, constantly struggling with each other. It is only when we find the time and space to truly encounter God that we can begin to change for the better.

How do you make up after such a massive disagreement? Jacob had fled from Esau and now, at least fifteen years later, he was thinking about going back. I know two brothers who fell out over the inheritance after their mum died. It ended with threats of violence, one brother moving away and the other brother talking some kind of a makeshift weapon (a golf umbrella or a walking stick) with him every time he went out. I could imagine Jacob and Esau in a similar situation. Jacob the trickster and Esau the angry are unlikely to ever be reconciled.

But the Lord did not abandon Jacob throughout all his struggles. God spoke to Jacob in a dream and reassured him that he would be made great, promising him that he would become wealthy. The Lord also tells Jacob when it is time for him to go home. Jacob obeys, setting out on his return journey. Although the Lord told Jacob to return, I doubt he was pleased with the manner of Jacob's departure: he sneaks away from Laban, and Rachel takes her father's household gods with her, presumably as an act of revenge against her father for his mistreatment of her husband. Laban never manages to recover them; Rachel conceals them from him when he chases after them and finally catches them up.

Laban and Jacob are reconciled at the second meeting. There is no clear apology, but they do make a covenant, promising to treat each other and their respective families well. This partial reconciliation stands as an interesting contrast to the fuller reconciliation which takes place between Jacob and Esau. There are a number of stages, recorded in Genesis 32 and 33. First Jacob sends messengers to notify Esau of his return. He hears that Esau is coming to meet him, accompanied by four hundred men. This scares Jacob, who divides his wealth in groups, hoping some at least will survive the attack he now believes to be immanent.

Jacob prays, a desperate prayer, begging God to keep him promise and preserve him from the expected devastation of Esau. But prayer alone is not enough; Jacob continues to make his own preparations. He sends Esau generous gifts: two hundred female and twenty male goats, thirty camels and their colts, forty cows and ten bulls, twenty female and ten male donkeys. All in all a vast herd, a big bribe to distract Esau from attacking Jacob. Most chilling of all, Jacob sends his family ahead of him, remaining alone for the evening. Perhaps he wanted to spare his family from his own fate? Perhaps they were one last attempt at distraction? It is impossible to know.

What we can be certain of is that it was during this lonely evening that the real transformation took place. What Jacob needed most was a change of heart, and that is what happened when he wrestled with God. Jacb begins the night in conflict with an unidentified stranger and it ends with him refusing to let go until he has received a blessing. I wonder if Jacob was preparing to die when he met Esau, and having given up all hope, all he wanted for the rest of his life was a final blessing before he died.

This experience completely changes him, from the trickster (*Jacob*) to the wrestler with God (*Israel*). He sees God face to face, naming the place of that encounter 'Face of God' (*Peniel*) as a reminder to himself.

We see Jacob's transformation into Israel in how he responds to his brother. Rather than hide behind his family, Israel goes ahead of them, preparing to face Esau himself. There is a tearful and joyful reunion; no violence, no recrimination. It appears the hard work of forgiveness has already taken place. The reconciliation is straightforward. The family are reunited and become one.

Unless we have wrestled with God, clung to him and let him break us and mould us to his will, we are unable to be agents of reconciliation in his world. Jacob the trickster was of little use to the God of compassion and mercy, but Israel, the wrestler with God, the one who clings to God, was his servant.

We all face conflict all of the time, and unless we are prepared to become agents of reconciliation, that conflict will sadly only increase. Jacob learnt the hard way about importance of forgiveness and reconciliation as means of dealing with conflict. This is also normally the case for each of us. There are easy ways, but we tend to prefer to make our own mistakes before learning that without costly forgiveness, there can be no peace.

Reflecting on the place of Christianity in Britain, in an article for the Daily Telegraph on 25th December 2013, A. N. Wilson commented that

> Yes, the hype and sentimentality surrounding the funeral of Nelson Mandela's were embarrassing, but at the core of it all was the central idea, embodied by a figure such as Archbishop Tutu, that it is possible to ignore the poison of hatred bubbling in your heart and forgive your enemies.

> The ANC, for long—yes—a terrorist organisation,
> changed its mind, and behaved, not like Jihadists,
> but like Christians. South Africa, riven as it is
> with every kind of human problem, got that thing
> right largely because Mandela in his prison years
> decided to risk all on what was a fundamentally
> Christian idea.

That fundamentally Christian idea is one summarised by Jesus himself in this way:

> 'You have heard that it was said, "Love your neigh-
> bour and hate your enemy." But I tell you, love
> your enemies and pray for those who persecute
> you, that you may be children of your Father in
> heaven. He causes his sun to rise on the evil and
> the good, and sends rain on the righteous and the
> unrighteous. If you love those who love you, what
> reward will you get?' (Matthew 5:43-46)

The Good News Jesus brought us is a message of forgive-ness, of peace, of an end to destructive conflict. We are not called simply to care for people like us, but to take the risk of caring for people who are not like us at all, to love those who make it so very hard for us to love them. Something that is completely impossible for us to do in our own strength, but more than possible in the power of God's Holy Spirit.

Story

The widow of a church organist who was beaten to death as he walked to Midnight Mass on Christmas Eve has said she forgives the men who killed him.

Alan Greaves suffered 'catastrophic' injuries when he was battered with a pick-axe handle in Sheffield on 24 December 2012.

On the night of the attack, the father-of-four had left his home in High Green, where his wife Maureen was with two of their children and twin grandchildren.

The 68-year-old retired social worker was making the short walk to St Saviour's Church to play the organ for the service, something he had done for 40 years.

But Mr. Greaves never arrived.

Instead, he crossed the path of two men who had gone out with the purpose of looking for someone to attack.

Ashley Foster, 22, was found guilty of manslaughter on 18th July 2013, in a trial at Sheffield Crown Court. Jonathan Bowling, also 22, had earlier admitted the killing.

Maureen Greaves said forgiving her husband's killers had been 'one of the hardest things' she had done.

'It seems so easy to say I've forgiven them, but it's probably one of the hardest things in my life that I've had to do and yet having done it and repeatedly seeking to do it, I've found I've benefited.

'I've not gone to bed with them on my mind, I've not gone around with shocking feelings over them, I've not gone over and over in my mind the replay of what happened to Alan.'

Mrs Greaves said she hoped both men would find 'some sense of true sorrow' for what they had done.

'Perhaps they'll find while they're in prison a journey they can go on where they will be able to think of what they've done and turn away from such things and start leading better lives.'

The end of the trial has closed a traumatic chapter for Mrs Greaves by finding those responsible for her husband's death.

She said: 'We're going to celebrate the end of the trial, we're going to celebrate his life and we're going to have a little cry because we do miss him as a family, not just me.'

Mrs Greaves said now the trial had finished, she was faced with a new chapter of 'getting down to really face singleness and the months and years ahead.'

The couple married in 1972 and dedicated much of their lives to church and community work.

As well as being an organist, Mr Greaves was a lay preacher at St Saviour's Church.

The couple also worked for the Church Army.

Mark Russell, its chief executive, said Mr Greaves' death had been an 'earthquake through the whole Church Army family.'

'Everyone in Church Army has rallied around Maureen and poured love and prayer and support into her life.'

Just weeks before his death, Mr Greaves had helped set up a new food bank project for people in Sheffield.

Mr Russell said: 'It seems almost cruel that he worked so hard to ensure everyone else had food on their table at Christmas when he wasn't around to enjoy his own.'

Questions for discussion

Unlike the previous four stories, the one above is entirely factual. It is based on an article from the BBC news website, altered only to include full dates. Maureen Greaves is one powerful example of a Christian who, despite terrible suffering, chose to forgive.

Forgiveness is a choice, an act of will, not an emotional state. Forgiveness is not forgetting. You can forgive without forgetting. Indeed you often have to forgive without forgetting, as Maureen Greaves and Nelson Mandela both showed. Forgiving does not mean that you must tolerate wrongdoing, or make excuses for behaviour that was, in fact, inexcusable. But if you chose to forgive, then you chose to not take revenge or demand repayment. That is to say, forgiveness means deciding to live with the consequences of another person's actions without taking revenge or demanding repayment.

The process of forgiving is a difficult and often painful one. But it is a necessary one, if we are to live as God intended us to.

1. Do you find it easy or difficult to forgive?

2. What about being forgiven?

3. How does the example of Maureen Greaves challenge you?

Read Genesis 32 and 33

1. What is good in Jacob's prayer? What is not so good?

2. What does the picture of wrestling with God suggest?

3. How has it changed Jacob?